Messages of

FINDING PURPOSE

for **Lent 2022**

Messages of

FINDING PURPOSE

for **Lent 2022**

3-MINUTE DEVOTIONS

MICHAEL WHITE and **TOM CORCORAN**

AVE MARIA PRESS AVE Notre Dame, Indiana

Founded in 1865, Ave Maria Press is a ministry of the United States Province of Holy Cross.

www.avemariapress.com

Paperback: ISBN-13 978-1-64680-105-3

E-book: ISBN-13 978-1-64680-106-0

Cover and text design by Samantha Watson.

Printed and bound in the United States of America.

Introduction

During his time spent as a prisoner in a Nazi concentration camp, Viktor Frankl carefully considered the meaning of life. He determined that our search for meaning and purpose runs far deeper than all our other desires. Somehow, we can undergo grueling trials and tribulations if we just come to grasp the purpose at the heart of it all.

Pastor Rick Warren made the same observation when he wrote the simple and astounding first line of his book *The Purpose Driven Life*: "It is not about you."

That line can be both a bit disconcerting and somewhat of a relief. It is disconcerting because we like to make life all about us. We love to place ourselves at the center of attention and have our will and our way. But it is also a relief because we know that when we make life about us, we most often end up all alone and on our own. We have been down that road and know it is a dead end.

Five hundred years before Christ, God spoke through the prophet Jeremiah to help us see the foolishness of finding our meaning and purpose in ourselves or any other human being. He wrote, "I know, LORD, that no one chooses their way, nor determines their course nor directs their own step" (Jer 10:23).

If you could summarize all of theology in one sentence, it would simply be this: there is a God, and we are not him. The beginning of wisdom is to start with God, who created us and knows his plan and purpose for us. We will not discover our purpose in ourselves; we find our purpose in our Creator. God is the almighty maker of heaven and earth, which means he is *our* maker; to find our purpose we have to start with him.

Jeremiah continues: "Correct me, LORD, but with equity, not in anger, lest you diminish me" (Jer 10:24).

Over time we can become distracted and drift away from God's purposes and plans for our lives. Other times, in our self-absorption, we can miss them altogether.

Lent serves as a time of correction and instruction. During Lent, we can make a concerted effort to again place God at the center of our lives. We undertake the Lenten journey to come to know God better, listening for his correction, seeking out his instruction and direction.

We pray that this Lent—through just a few minutes of reflection and prayer each day—you will connect with your Creator and claim a clearer sense of purpose. As you invest in his Word and his purposes, may you grow in faith, hope, and love.

Fr. Michael and Tom
Church of the Nativity, Timonium, Maryland

WEEK OF
Ash Wednesday

Wednesday, March 2
Ash Wednesday

So we are ambassadors for Christ, as if God were appealing through us. We implore you on behalf of Christ, be reconciled to God.

—2 Corinthians 5:20

As we enter this season of Lent, Paul reminds us that we are "ambassadors for Christ." We have been made spokespersons for Christ by Baptism and so our words, thoughts, and actions need to reflect this to all whom we meet. That is our purpose in life, to be Christ's presence in our world.

....

Pray today for the gift of courage to be an ambassador for Christ and for his help in learning just how he wants you to do that.

Thursday, March 3

I have set before you life and death, the blessing and the curse. Choose life, then, that you and your descendants may live, by loving the LORD, your God, obeying his voice, and holding fast to him.
—Deuteronomy 30:19–20

Moses tells the Israelites to choose life so that they and their descendants will enjoy abundant life. The way to choose life is to cling to the Lord, loving him and listening to what he has to say to us.

....

What do you think God is saying to you in the quiet of your heart and in the gathered community of the Church? Pray to Jesus to help you understand the Father's voice and to hold fast to him in faith.

Friday, March 4

Then [Jesus] said to all, "If anyone wishes to come after me, he must deny himself and take up his cross daily and follow me."

—Luke 9:23

As we look ahead to the first full week of Lent, we hear Jesus reminding us of the cost of discipleship: to take up our cross each day and follow him. With Christ all things are possible, so we need not run in fear from whatever cross might lay ahead of us. If we cling to the Father and follow Jesus closely, we will know eternal life.

....

Write down one cross you need to carry in your life right now. Put the note somewhere and remember to pray about your cross each day until Easter. Ask Jesus to help you carry your cross and to understand the purpose of it in your life right now.

Saturday, March 5

Psalm 25:4–9

Your ways, O Lord, are love and truth to those who keep your covenant.

Your ways, O Lᴏʀᴅ, make known to me;
    teach me your paths.
Guide me in your truth and teach me,
    for you are God my savior.

Your ways, O Lord, are love and truth to those who keep your covenant.

Remember that your compassion, O Lᴏʀᴅ,
    and your love are from of old.
In your kindness remember me,
    because of your goodness, O Lᴏʀᴅ.

Your ways, O Lord, are love and truth to those who keep your covenant.

Good and upright is the Lᴏʀᴅ,
    thus he shows sinners the way.
He guides the humble to justice,
    and he teaches the humble his way.

Your ways, O Lord, are love and truth to those who keep your covenant.

FIRST WEEK

OF LENT

Sunday, March 6

Have you ever wondered, *Why am I here?* Exploring this very important question throughout Lent this year will help us look at our purpose in life and grapple with just why we are here.

Knowing our "why" provides purpose and meaning and adds value to our lives. It will get us through the difficult times and make the good times far more enjoyable. Most important, if we are to have a life of meaning and significance, if we are to flourish, we need to know why we are here. It would be a tragedy to go through life not knowing why we were put on this earth.

To understand our why, we start with God. God is our Maker and Creator. God has set eternity in our hearts. He has placed in us a longing for something more than just existing—a deeper purpose beyond the day-to-day busyness of life.

....

Pray for the grace to know God's purpose and meaning for your life. Pray that during this Lenten season, you will come to understand more fully what God has already put in your heart.

Monday, March 7

And [Jesus] told [his disciples] a parable, "Can a blind person guide a blind person? Will not both fall into a pit? No disciple is superior to the teacher; but when fully trained, every disciple will be like his teacher."

—Luke 6:39–40

This passage from Luke is taken from the Sermon on the Plain. Jesus asks a rhetorical question and then answers it. If a blind person leads a blind person, then both are liable to fall or fail. He continues this train of thought. Each of us will follow someone. We will look to someone to teach us how to live. And we will become most like the person we follow and who teaches us about life.

We are all disciples of someone. We all look to someone to show us the meaning and purpose of life. It makes sense to turn to Jesus, the author of life, as our teacher. In comparison to Jesus, other teachers are blind. They cannot see with the insight of the Son of God. Jesus has the authority to lead us to a life of meaning and purpose.

....

Think about who you have been following. Ask God to help you instead follow Jesus and seek out his purpose for you.

Tuesday, March 8

A good tree does not bear rotten fruit, nor does a rotten tree bear good fruit. For every tree is known by its own fruit. For people do not pick figs from thornbushes, nor do they gather grapes from brambles.

—Luke 6:43–44

Jesus uses an analogy here to talk about human nature and the human condition. A good tree does not produce rotten fruit. A healthy tree produces good fruit, and a rotten tree produces rotten fruit. Thornbushes cannot produce figs, and brambles cannot produce grapes.

What is true of nature is true for human beings. We often think that the way to produce healthy fruit is to focus on our actions, on what we are doing. Jesus challenges us instead to look at our hearts and internal motivations. If we are healthy on the inside, then good fruit will come out of us. When we connect with Jesus, we are transformed from the inside out so that we will produce good fruit.

....

Pray today that Jesus will change and transform you from the inside out.

Wednesday, March 9

A good person out of the store of goodness in his heart produces good, but an evil person out of a store of evil produces evil; for from the fullness of the heart the mouth speaks.

—Luke 6:45

Jesus continues to teach that what comes out of us comes from what is inside of us. Good actions come out of good people, and evil actions come out of people who are corrupted at their core. Further, what we say is a reflection of our hearts. If we find sarcasm and criticism and negative speech coming out of our mouths, it reveals the need for our hearts to be cleansed and transformed.

....

Pay attention to the words that come out of your mouth today. What do those words reveal about your heart? Ask God to purify your heart so that better speech comes out of your mouth.

Thursday, March 10

Cursed is the man who trusts in human beings, who makes flesh his strength, whose heart turns away from the LORD. He is like a barren bush in the wasteland that enjoys no change of season, but stands in lava beds in the wilderness, a land, salty and uninhabited.

—Jeremiah 17:5–6

Jeremiah warns that when we put our trust in human beings or look to them for our meaning and purpose, we are cursed. This may sound harsh, but it simply means that it will not work out for us if we seek to understand our purpose from other human beings.

Jeremiah then gives a word picture of what it is like to trust in human beings for our purpose. We are like a tree in a desert that has no access to water or nutrients in the soil. It withers and dries up. We will also dry up and wither when we look to human beings for our meaning and purpose.

....

Pray today for the grace to look to God and his purposes for your meaning and significance.

Friday, March 11

Blessed are those who trust in the Lord; the Lord will be their trust. They are like a tree planted beside the waters that stretches out its roots to the stream: It does not fear heat when it comes, its leaves stay green; In the year of drought it shows no distress, but still produces fruit.

—Jeremiah 17:7–8

Jeremiah says that blessed is the person who trusts in the Lord or who looks to the Lord for meaning and purpose in life. We are like a tree planted next to a stream of water. It has constant access to water. It finds nutrients in the soil. It does not have to worry about the external world because internally it is healthy.

We become healthy internally when we find our meaning and purpose in the Lord and not from something or someone else. We do not have to fear difficult times because we find a source of strength in the Lord.

....

Pray today for the grace to find your meaning and purpose in the Lord and not from the world.

Saturday, March 12

Psalm 86:1–6

Teach me your way, O Lord, that I may walk in your truth.

Incline your ear, O LORD answer me,
    for I am afflicted and poor.
Keep my life, for I am devoted to you;
    save your servant who trusts in you.
You are my God.

Teach me your way, O Lord, that I may walk in your truth.

Have mercy on me, O Lord,
    for to you I call all the day.
Gladden the soul of your servant,
    for to you, O Lord, I lift up my soul.

Teach me your way, O Lord, that I may walk in your truth.

For you, O Lord, are good and forgiving,
    abounding in kindness to all who call upon
        you.
Hearken, O LORD, to my prayer
    and attend to the sound of my pleading.

Teach me your way, O Lord, that I may walk in your truth.

Second Week

OF LENT

Sunday, March 13

The word "worship" comes from the Old English word "worth-ship," which meant worthy, valuable, and worth something. You worship whatever you believe will bring value and meaning to your life.

Worship is the first purpose of our lives because it is the foundation of all the other ones. If we are going to live for God and find our meaning and purpose in him, we must decide to worship him. If we don't worship God, we will find ourselves worshipping something or someone else.

Pray today that, through the course of this week, you will grow in your worship of God.

Monday, March 14

Filled with the holy Spirit, Jesus returned from the Jordan and was led by the Spirit into the desert for forty days, to be tempted by the devil.

—Luke 4:1–2

The Holy Spirit leads Jesus out into the desert for forty days, where he would be tempted by the devil. Jesus experiences temptation even though he hadn't done anything wrong. In fact, he experiences temptation because he was doing something right.

Sometimes we can put ourselves in an environment that tempts us to do wrong. We choose situations that are not good for us. Whenever possible, we should avoid temptation; other times, we might be doing the right thing and still be tempted. Experiencing temptation doesn't make us bad—it makes us human.

We will be tempted to make something other than God our number one priority over and over again throughout our lives. This is part of the human condition.

....

Pray for the grace to overcome the temptation today to put something or someone before God.

Tuesday, March 15

He ate nothing during those days, and when they were over he was hungry. The devil said to him, "If you are the Son of God, command this stone to become bread." Jesus answered him, "It is written, 'One does not live by bread alone.'"

—Luke 4:2–4

Jesus goes out into the desert to fast for forty days and forty nights. This shows Jesus' incredible strength and discipline that he could go without food for so long. Now he is hungry, so the devil tempts him to meet his legitimate need for food in an illegitimate way.

Notice also how the devil starts the temptation, "If you are the Son of God." The devil tempts Jesus to doubt his identity, to doubt his relationship with his heavenly Father. This is how temptation often comes to us. We are tempted to doubt our connection to God and whether we can really trust him to meet our needs.

....

Pray for the grace today to place your trust in God to meet your needs.

Wednesday, March 16

Then he took him up and showed him all the kingdoms of the world in a single instant. The devil said to him, "I shall give to you all this power and their glory; for it has been handed over to me, and I may give it to whomever I wish. All this will be yours, if you worship me." Jesus said to him in reply, "It is written: 'You shall worship the Lord, your God, and him alone shall you serve.'"

—Luke 4:5–8

The devil takes Jesus and shows him all the kingdoms of the world and says that they can be his if Jesus will simply bow down and worship him. Jesus came for the purpose to win back the kingdoms of the world for God. It was the mission he came to achieve. The devil is tempting Jesus not with a bad thing but with something very good. In that moment, Jesus had to determine what was most important: his relationship with his Father or the mission to win back all the kingdoms of the world.

We worship what we view as the most important thing in our lives. And there can only be one number one. We will worship whatever we believe brings the most value and significance to our lives. Jesus reminds us we are to make God the number one priority of our lives—not power, not pleasures, not possessions, not kids, and not sports.

....

Pray today for the grace to make God your number one priority.

Thursday, March 17

I urge you therefore, brothers, by the mercies of God, to offer your bodies as a living sacrifice, holy and pleasing to God, your spiritual worship.
—Romans 12:1

Paul tells us to offer our bodies and lives as a living sacrifice that is holy and pleasing to God. When we do this, it is worship. Worship of God begins at Mass, but it does not end there. We worship God whenever we offer him our activities and abilities.

Every human activity, except sin, can be done for God's pleasure and glory if you do it with an attitude of praise. You can wash dishes, sell a product, write a computer program, weed your garden, and raise a family for the glory of God. Like a proud parent, God especially enjoys watching you use the talents and abilities he has given you.

Take a moment to offer your day to God. In your mind, go through your plans and activities for today. Offer every one up to God in this time of prayer.

Friday, March 18

Do not store up for yourselves treasures on earth, where moth and decay destroy, and thieves break in and steal. But store up treasures in heaven, where neither moth nor decay destroys, nor thieves break in and steal. For where your treasure is, there also will your heart be.

—Matthew 6:19–21

Jesus tells us that where our treasure is, our heart will also be. This is just a principle of life. Wherever you spend your money gets a little piece of your heart. You begin to care about it.

This is why we are encouraged to give to our place of worship as an act of worship. If we fail to make an intentional offering to God, we hold back some of our heart from him. Every time we give, we are expressing trust in God and giving him more of our heart and lives.

....

Take a moment to reread the verse above. Pray for the grace to give to God in such a way that it grows your love and trust in him.

Saturday, March 19

Psalm 119:1–2, 4–5, 7–8

Blessed are they who follow the law of the Lord!

Blessed are they whose way is blameless,
    who walk in the law of the LORD.
Blessed are they who observe his decrees,
    who seek him with all their heart.

Blessed are they who follow the law of the Lord!

You have commanded that your precepts
    be diligently kept.
Oh, that I might be firm in the ways
    of keeping your statutes!

Blessed are they who follow the law of the Lord!

I will give you thanks with an upright heart,
    when I have learned your just ordinances.
I will keep your statutes;
    do not utterly forsake me.

Blessed are they who follow the law of the Lord!

THIRD WEEK

OF LENT

Sunday, March 20

In the scriptures, God reveals five purposes for our lives, ways we access the life he has for us: worship, fellowship, discipleship, ministry, and evangelization or mission.

This week, we are going to look at fellowship. The purpose of fellowship means that we are formed for God's family. God has created you to be part of his family. God has created you to call him your heavenly Father. And all other Christ followers are to be our brothers and sisters in Christ.

....

Thank God today that he has made you a part of his family. Pray that this week you will come to a greater understanding of the blessings and responsibilities of being in God's family.

Monday, March 21

[Jesus] took Peter, John, and James and went up the mountain to pray. While he was praying his face changed in appearance and his clothing became dazzling white. And behold, two men were conversing with him, Moses and Elijah, who appeared in glory and spoke of his exodus that he was going to accomplish in Jerusalem.

—Luke 9:28b–31

Jesus formed a community and lived his life in it. He gathered twelve apostles who were his friends and followers. Many times, Jesus would go to pray by himself, but here he takes his three closest apostles. They go up to the mountain to pray and connect with God. While praying, Jesus' clothes become dazzling white. Moses and Elijah—the two greatest prophets of the Old Testament—appear before Jesus, conversing with him and in community with him.

Jesus continues to build communities of people. He wants to connect us with other followers so we will have support in our faith. We need a community of people that pray together and help us on our life's journey.

....

Today in your prayer time, acknowledge your need for friends in faith. Thank Jesus that he wants to provide them for you.

Tuesday, March 22

Peter and his companions had been overcome by sleep, but becoming fully awake, they saw his glory and the two men standing with him. As they were about to part from him, Peter said to Jesus, "Master, it is good that we are here; let us make three tents, one for you, one for Moses, and one for Elijah." But he did not know what he was saying.
—Luke 9:32–33

Peter didn't know what he was talking about, but that never stopped him from speaking. Apparently saying nothing wasn't an option for him. Peter suggests the group just stays on the mountain and lives there. God gives us mountaintop experiences to fuel us, but we cannot live there.

Jesus hadn't brought Peter, James, and John up the mountain so they could stay there. He brought them up the mountain because they were his close friends and confidants. He shared more of his life with them than with anyone else. He wants them to know something about him that no one else knows. Jesus had to carry this burden of his identity as the Son of God and Savior of the world all on his own.

We all have burdens or facts about our lives that the world at large does not know. That is healthy, but we need a few people who know what is beneath the surface. We need two or three friends in faith who know us inside and out.

....

Who are the people who really know you? Thank God for them today. If you can't name anyone, ask God to send those people into your life.

Wednesday, March 23

While he was still speaking, a cloud came and cast a shadow over them, and they became frightened when they entered the cloud. Then from the cloud came a voice that said, "This is my chosen Son; listen to him." After the voice had spoken, Jesus was found alone. They fell silent and did not at that time tell anyone what they had seen.

—Luke 9:34–36

As Peter was speaking, a cloud came. The cloud represented the presence of the Holy Spirit. Then the voice of God the Father said, "This is my chosen Son; listen to him." In this moment, even more about Jesus was revealed. Jesus is God's Son, and the apostles should listen to him. Then in an instant it was all gone. The apostles got a glimpse of Jesus' divine nature, and then the vision ended. The apostles didn't tell anyone what they had seen.

A big part of being a close friend in faith is that we keep confidences. When someone shares with us their struggles or problems, we keep them in confidence. When someone shares their heart, we honor them by keeping what we know about them to ourselves.

....

Who are the people who trust you with their hearts? Pray for them and thank God that they trust you. Pray that you would honor that trust.

Thursday, March 24

[Jesus] came and preached peace to you who were far off and peace to those who were near, for through him we both have access in one Spirit to the Father. So then you are no longer strangers and sojourners, but you are fellow citizens with the holy ones and members of the household of God, built upon the foundation of the apostles and prophets, with Christ Jesus as the capstone.

—Ephesians 2:17–20

Paul writes to the Ephesians and reminds them that they are no longer traveling aimlessly through life. They can have peace with God. They know that they belong to God and to his household.

The same is true for us. We have been formed for God's family. This means we can find our identity as beloved sons and daughters of God.

....

Thank God today that he has formed you for his family. You have a place where you belong.

Friday, March 25
Solemnity of the
Annunciation of the Lord

Therefore, putting away falsehood, speak the truth,
each one to his neighbor, for we are members one
of another.

—Ephesians 4:25

Paul writes to the Ephesians and tells them how to live in Christian community. He is writing about how to have a healthy community. Paul writes that we are to put away all falsehood. Falsehood includes lying, but it means more than that. It includes being fake or inauthentic.

Paul goes on to say we are to speak the truth to other members of the Church. We are to be honest with others even when the truth is painful. The reason we are honest and speak hard truths is that we belong to one another. We are connected to one another. If we are being false or untruthful to others, we are, in a sense, lying to ourselves.

....

At the Annunciation, the archangel Gabriel speaks the truth of God's plan to Mary, which greatly troubles her at first. Speaking the truth can be incredibly difficult. Pray today for the grace to speak the truth to your close friends in faith. Pray that honesty characterizes all of your relationships.

Saturday, March 26

Psalm 103:1–4, 9–10, 11–12
The Lord is kind and merciful.
Bless the LORD, O my soul;
    and all my being, bless his holy name.
Bless the LORD, O my soul,
    and forget not all his benefits.
The Lord is kind and merciful.
He pardons all your iniquities,
    he heals all your ills.
He redeems your life from destruction,
    he crowns you with kindness and compassion.
The Lord is kind and merciful.
He will not always chide,
    nor does he keep his wrath forever.
Not according to our sins does he deal with us,
    nor does he requite us according to our crimes.
The Lord is kind and merciful.
For as the heavens are high above the earth,
    so surpassing is his kindness toward those who
        fear him.
As far as the east is from the west,
    so far has he put our transgressions from us.
The Lord is kind and merciful.

Fourth Week

OF LENT

Sunday, March 27

We have been made to live in eternity with God, and so the purpose of this life is to begin living that life right now. We are to live in light of God's purposes.

This week, we are looking at the purpose of discipleship. We have been created to be like Christ in character. We are to become people who do what Jesus would do in our situation. Becoming like Christ requires that we make efforts to grow more like him. However, becoming like Christ is not something that comes from our own work—rather, we cooperate with God's grace in striving to become who he intends us to be.

....

In your prayer time today, tell God that you want to become like his Son in your character.

Monday, March 28

We know that all things work for good for those who love God, who are called according to his purpose. For those he foreknew he also predestined to be conformed to the image of his Son, so that he might be the firstborn among many brothers.
—Romans 8:28–29

Paul tells the Romans that God works in every situation for those who love him and have a relationship with him. God works to bring about change and growth in our character. God's grace is at work to conform us to the image of his Son. God is at work to conform our character into Christ's character. Jesus is meant to be the first of God's many sons and daughters who reflect God's image.

Jesus is the model. We have been created to become like Christ and act as he would act if he were in our shoes. As Rick Warren writes, "God's ultimate goal for your life is not comfort, but character development."

Ask God to show you today how he wants you to become more like his Son so that you are more conformed to his image.

Tuesday, March 29

Meanwhile Moses was tending the flock of his father-in-law Jethro, the priest of Midian. Leading the flock beyond the wilderness, he came to the mountain of God, Horeb. There the angel of the Lord appeared to him as fire flaming out of a bush. When he looked, although the bush was on fire, it was not being consumed. So Moses decided, "I must turn aside to look at this remarkable sight. Why does the bush not burn up?"

—Exodus 3:1–3

Exodus tells us that Moses was going through his daily routine as a shepherd for his father-in-law. To get his attention, God gave him a sign. He showed him a burning bush that was not consumed. Moses could have ignored the sign, but he decided to turn aside from his daily routine to examine the sign.

To become like Christ, we must decide that we want it to be a purpose for our lives. We are often consumed with goals and projects or having a good time. Becoming like Christ does not mean ignoring tasks or not enjoying ourselves, but it does mean deciding to care more about our character than our achievements, our comfort, or our pleasure.

....

Tell God that you want to become like his Son. Ask for the grace to overcome the temptations to make comfort, fun, popularity, or achievement more important.

Wednesday, March 30

> Remain in me, as I remain in you. Just as a branch cannot bear fruit on its own unless it remains on the vine, so neither can you unless you remain in me. I am the vine, you are the branches. Whoever remains in me and I in him will bear much fruit, because without me you can do nothing.
>
> —John 15:4–5

Jesus tells the apostles to abide in him, to simply stay connected to him. He then uses the analogy of a branch on a fruit tree. The branch cannot bear fruit all alone, cut off from the rest of the tree. It bears fruit because it receives water and nutrients from the tree. In the same way, change in our characters comes not from us but from God.

Becoming like Christ in our character happens as we abide in the person of Jesus Christ. This means simply staying connected to Jesus. How do we do that? Daily prayer and the sacraments are the best ways in which we abide in or stay connected to Christ. Another way is calling Jesus to mind through simple little prayers, such as "Jesus, Son of God, have mercy on me." Or saying, "Jesus, you are my savior and deliverer."

....

Take a moment to be with Jesus. Repeat one of the short prayers above and then pray it throughout the day.

Thursday, March 31

So then, my beloved, obedient as you have always been, not only when I am present but all the more now that I am absent, work out your salvation with fear and trembling. For God is the one who, for his good purpose, works in you both to desire and to work. Do everything without grumbling or questioning.

—Philippians 2:12–14

Paul encourages the Philippians to continue in their obedience of God. He tells them to work out their salvation with fear and trembling. Our salvation needs to be worked out in the details of our lives. Our salvation simply means to have Christ's character formed in us so we become who God created us to be. While it is God who changes us, we have to choose to cooperate with God's grace.

We have to work with God's grace to change. The good news is that God is working within us to help us to cooperate. Even in our efforts to change, it is never just us alone but God's grace aiding us and helping us to become more like his Son.

....

Work out your salvation by doing all things without grumbling or questioning. For just today, try to do everything with joy and obedience to God so that you are like his Son.

Friday, April 1

Beloved, we are God's children now; what we shall be has not yet been revealed. We do know that when it is revealed we shall be like him, for we shall see him as he is. Everyone who has this hope based on him makes himself pure, as he is pure.

—1 John 3:2–3

John tells us that we are God's children. As children of God, we are still growing in our maturity. We are not yet conformed to the image of his Son. We are in the process of becoming more the people God has created us to be. This means we are to continue to purify ourselves by discarding the sin in our lives and what keeps us from becoming like Christ in our character.

....

Today, talk to God the Father. Confess your need to grow and mature to become like his Son. Ask the Holy Spirit to show you what you need to discard today.

Saturday, April 2

Psalm 51:3–4, 18–19, 20–21

It is mercy I desire, and not sacrifice.

Have mercy on me, O God, in your goodness;
    in the greatness of your compassion wipe out
        my offense.
Thoroughly wash me from my guilt
    and of my sin cleanse me.

It is mercy I desire, and not sacrifice.

For you are not pleased with sacrifices;
    should I offer a burnt offering, you would not
        accept it.
My sacrifice, O God, is a contrite spirit;
    a heart contrite and humbled, O God, you will
        not spurn.

It is mercy I desire, and not sacrifice.

Be bountiful, O LORD, to Zion in your kindness
    by rebuilding the walls of Jerusalem;
Then shall you be pleased with due sacrifices,
    burnt offerings and holocausts.

It is mercy I desire, and not sacrifice.

Fifth Week

OF LENT

Sunday, April 3

We continue looking at the purposes God has given us in order to live in light of eternity. We have reflected on worship, fellowship, discipleship, and ministry. The fifth purpose is mission. We have been made for a mission. We have been made to impact the world for Christ. Our mission is to bring God's love to people in the world so they can connect with the person of Jesus Christ.

God wants you to have a ministry in the Body of Christ and a mission out in the world. He wants you serving your church family and also serving the larger human family. Jesus calls us to come to him and go out into the world for him.

Over and over again throughout the gospels, we see that Jesus cares for people who do not know his heavenly Father and would have been outsiders to the religious system. He reached out to people whose choices seemed to disqualify them from a relationship with God. And he reached out to people lacking in material resources.

....

Today, pray to see the opportunities around you to bring God's love to people who do not know it.

Monday, April 4

Jesus went to the Mount of Olives. But early in the morning he arrived again in the temple area, and all the people started coming to him, and he sat down and taught them.

—John 8:1–2

Throughout his public ministry, even as it drew to a close with his approaching death, Jesus gave witness to the faith and taught his friends and followers to do the same. This means they are to be a witness of what God has done for them through the whole of their lives and wherever they find themselves.

A witness doesn't make an argument. A witness simply shares his or her experience. As followers of Christ, we fulfill the purpose of mission when we share what God has done for us. We have opportunities in everyday life in our work and families, and we can even reach the ends of the earth now through the power of the internet.

....

Ask God today to show you the opportunities you have on a regular basis to be a witness to his love.

Tuesday, April 5

> They said to him, "Teacher, this woman was caught in the very act of committing adultery. Now in the law, Moses commanded us to stone such a woman. So what do you say?" They said this to test him, so that they could have some charge to bring against him. Jesus bent down and began to write on the ground with his finger. But when they continued asking him, he straightened up and said to them, "Let the one among you who is without sin be the first to throw a stone at her." Again he bent down and wrote on the ground.
>
> —John 8:4–8

The religious leaders try to trap Jesus. They know he has taught on love and compassion for sinners, prostitutes, and tax collectors, so they know stoning the woman would contradict his own values and teaching. However, the Law of Moses said that anyone caught in adultery should be stoned.

Jesus appears trapped, but instead of falling directly into the trap, Jesus challenges the religious leaders. He says that whoever is without sin and perfect can cast the first stone. Jesus consistently challenged religious insiders, especially when they wanted to point to the sins of outsiders.

....

Pray today to avoid the sin of being judgmental to people who act apart from God. Pray for the grace to reflect Jesus' heart to people who are not connected to Christ and his Church.

Wednesday, April 6

And in response, they went away one by one, beginning with the elders. So he was left alone with the woman before him. Then Jesus straightened up and said to her, "Woman, where are they? Has no one condemned you?" She replied, "No one, sir." Then Jesus said, "Neither do I condemn you. Go, [and] from now on do not sin any more."

—John 8:9–11

When Jesus challenges the religious leaders to consider their own sins, they all leave one by one so that Jesus is left alone with the woman. Jesus alone had the right to condemn her since he was sinless and perfect. Instead he comforts the woman and encourages her to sin no more.

Jesus challenged insiders and comforted outsiders. We are to have the same heart as Jesus. We should comfort and accept outsiders and then encourage them on the right path.

....

Do you know someone who is going down the wrong path and, by their daily choices, is walking away from God? Pray for him or her today. Pray for the grace to be a witness of God's love for them.

Thursday, April 7

Jesus went around to all the towns and villages, teaching in their synagogues, proclaiming the gospel of the kingdom, and curing every disease and illness. At the sight of the crowds, his heart was moved with pity for them because they were troubled and abandoned, like sheep without a shepherd.

—Matthew 9:35–36

Jesus went about preaching and teaching about the kingdom of God, and he healed people of their illnesses and diseases. Despite all his work, he saw that there was still so much more to do. He saw people in pain and hurting. He saw their pain, and he had compassion on them because they did not have a spiritual leader to lead them.

Living out our mission means seeing the pain in others and having compassion for them. Many people are going the wrong direction because they lack strong spiritual leadership. They need the witness of a good follower of Christ. Other people are suffering because of their immediate environment or because they lack access to the resources required for a good life.

....

Whose suffering do you see that fills you with compassion to do something about it? Ask God how he wants you to respond this week.

Friday, April 8

At the sight of the crowds, his heart was moved with pity for them because they were troubled and abandoned, like sheep without a shepherd. Then he said to his disciples, "The harvest is abundant but the laborers are few; so ask the master of the harvest to send out laborers for his harvest."

—Matthew 9:37–38

Jesus sees the pain of the disciples and has compassion on them because they don't have any spiritual leaders. Then he tells the apostles to pray to the Lord of the harvest to send out laborers to the harvest.

We are the laborers God sends out into the harvest. We are sent out to be spiritual leaders in our community so we can draw people into a relationship with our heavenly Father. If you are a follower of Christ, you are a spiritual leader to the people in your work, family, and community.

....

Ask God to help you to see yourself as a spiritual leader and to lead the people around you to him.

Saturday, April 9

Jeremiah 31:10–13

The Lord will guard us, as a shepherd guards his flock.

Hear the word of the LORD, O nations,
    proclaim it on distant isles, and say:
He who scattered Israel, now gathers them togeth-
    er, he guards them as a shepherd his flock.

The Lord will guard us, as a shepherd guards his flock.

The LORD shall ransom Jacob,
    he shall redeem him from the hand of his
        conqueror.
Shouting, they shall mount the heights of Zion,
    they shall come streaming to the LORD's
        blessings:
The grain, the wine, and the oil,
    the sheep and the oxen.

The Lord will guard us, as a shepherd guards his flock.

Then the virgins shall make merry and dance,
    and young men and old as well.
I will turn their mourning into joy,
I will console and gladden them after their sorrows.

The Lord will guard us, as a shepherd guards his flock.

HOLY WEEK

Sunday, April 10
Palm Sunday of the Passion of the Lord

Today we enter holy week and complete our Lenten journey. Our journey leads to the Cross of Christ as we remember that Jesus laid down his life so we might have life. Throughout this week, we will be reflecting on the Cross of Christ and what Jesus accomplished for us.

....

Ask Jesus to help you grow this week in your appreciation for his work on the Cross.

Monday, April 11

The LORD spoke to Moses and said to him: Tell your brother Aaron that he is not to come whenever he pleases into the inner sanctuary, inside the veil, in front of the cover on the ark, lest he die.
—Leviticus 16:1–2

In the Tabernacle of the Exodus, and later in the Temple in Jereusalem, there was a place called the Holy of Holies. This was an inner sanctum where the presence of God was said to dwell with the people of Israel. Only the high priest could enter into this place and only once a year on the Day of Atonement. The Holy of Holies was set apart with a huge curtain that was inches thick and dozens of feet tall. It was a symbol of the great divide between God and man because of the debt we owed God due to sin.

When Jesus died, this curtain was torn in two from top to bottom. God tore the veil of the temple to show that the divide no longer exists. The debt has been canceled by Jesus' death on the Cross.

....

Thank Jesus for paying your debt so you can freely enter into a relationship with your heavenly Father.

Tuesday, April 12

At noon darkness came over the whole land until three in the afternoon. Ad at three o'clock Jesus cried out in loud voice, "*Eloi, Eloi, lema sabach-thani?*" which is translated, "My God, my God, why have you forsaken me?"

—Mark 15:33–34

Sin brings about a threefold alienation or separation. Sin separates us from ourselves as we no longer feel comfortable in our own skin. Sin alienates us from other people; we are at war with others. And sin alienates us from God. Jesus on the Cross felt the full weight of this alienation. He was abandoned by his closest friends and then felt the separation from his heavenly Father.

Jesus, who never sinned, experienced the pain of sin so that we could have a relationship with our heavenly Father.

....

Thank Jesus today for experiencing that alienation so that you could live in relationship with God and others.

Wednesday, April 13

Now one of the criminals hanging there reviled Jesus, saying, "Are you not the Messiah? Save yourself and us." The other, however, rebuking him, said in reply, "Have you no fear of God, for you are subject to the same condemnation? And indeed, we have been condemned justly, for the sentence we received corresponds to our crimes, but this man has done nothing criminal." Then he said, "Jesus, remember me when you come into your kingdom." He replied to him, "Amen, I say to you, today you will be with me in Paradise."

—Luke 23:39–43

People who were crucified ultimately died from suffocation. As you hung on the cross, fluid would pour into your lungs. A man hanging on a cross had to continually pull himself up, just to catch a breath. For every breath Jesus took on the cross, he had to expend a great deal of energy. It cost Jesus dearly to answer the other criminal on the cross.

The criminal crucified alongside Jesus was a thief. He deserved to die, as he noted, according to the law, but by simply asking Jesus to remember him in his kingdom, he receives eternal life.

We cannot earn eternal life. We cannot earn the paradise of heaven. We can't earn it, but we can receive it because of Jesus' work on the Cross.

....

Take a moment to pray with the Good Thief. Pray today, "Jesus, remember me when you come into your kingdom."

Thursday, April 14
Holy Thursday

There they crucified him, and with him two others,
one on either side, with Jesus in the middle. Pilate
also had an inscription written and put on the cross.
It read, "Jesus the Nazorean, the King of the Jews."
—John 19:18–19

When the Romans crucified a man, they would put
the charge over his head. Pilate writes that Jesus is
the King of the Jews. Jesus had resisted this title
throughout his ministry and even through his trial,
but here on the Cross, Jesus is proclaimed king.

Jesus is proclaimed king on the Cross when he
performs his ultimate act of service for us. He uses
his kingship not to control and manipulate others
but to serve us and bring us into a relationship
with his Father.

....

Take a moment to acknowledge Christ as your king.
Thank him for his work and service on the Cross.

Friday, April 15
Good Friday

When Jesus had taken the wine, he said, "It is finished." And bowing his head, he handed over the
spirit.

—John 19:30

Before Jesus dies on the Cross, he says, "It is finished." He doesn't mean he is finished, but that
his redemptive work has been completed. He fully
surrendered his life in order to pay our debt.

....

Thank Jesus today for surrendering his life so that you
may have life.

Saturday, April 16
Holy Saturday

Psalm 104:1–2, 5–6, 10–12, 13–14

Lord, send out your Spirit, and renew the face of the earth.

Bless the LORD, O my soul!
O LORD, my God, you are great indeed!
You are clothed with majesty and glory,
    robed in light as with a cloak.

Lord, send out your Spirit, and renew the face of the earth.

You fixed the earth upon its foundation,
    not to be moved forever;
with the ocean, as with a garment, you covered it;
    above the mountains the waters stood.

Lord, send out your Spirit, and renew the face of the earth.

You send forth springs into the watercourses
    that wind among the mountains.
Beside them the birds of heaven dwell;
    from among the branches they send forth their
        song.

Lord, send out your Spirit, and renew the face of the earth.

You water the mountains from your palace;
    the earth is replete with the fruit of your works.
You raise grass for the cattle,
    and vegetation for man's use,
Producing bread from the earth.

Lord, send out your Spirit, and renew the face of the earth.
How manifold are your works, O LORD!
In wisdom you have wrought them all—
    the earth is full of your creatures.
Bless the LORD, O my soul! Alleluia.
Lord, send out your Spirit, and renew the face of the earth.

Fr. Michael White is a priest of the Archdiocese of Baltimore and pastor of Church of the Nativity in Timonium, Maryland. White is the coauthor of *Rebuilt*—which narrates the story of Nativity's rebirth—*Tools for Rebuilding, Rebuilding Your Message, The Rebuilt Field Guide*, and *ChurchMoney*. He is also coauthor of the bestselling Messages series for Advent and Lent.

During White's tenure as pastor at Church of the Nativity, the church has almost tripled in weekend attendance. More importantly, commitment to the mission of the Church has grown, demonstrated by the significant increase of giving and service in ministry, and much evidence of genuine spiritual renewal.

White earned his bachelor's degree from Loyola University Maryland and his graduate degrees in sacred theology and ecclesiology from the Pontifical Gregorian University in Rome.

Tom Corcoran has served Church of the Nativity in Timonium, Maryland, in a variety of roles that give him a unique perspective on parish ministry and leadership. First hired as a youth minister, Corcoran has also served as coordinator of children's ministry and director of small groups. He is lay associate to the pastor and is responsible for weekend message development, strategic planning, and staff development.

Corcoran is the coauthor of *Rebuilt*—which narrates the story of Nativity's rebirth—*Tools for Rebuilding, Rebuilding Your Message, The Rebuilt Field Guide*, and *ChurchMoney*. He is also coauthor of the bestselling Messages series for Advent and Lent.

churchnativity.com
rebuiltparish.com
rebuiltparish.podbean.com

Facebook: churchnativity
Twitter: @churchnativity
Instagram: @churchnativity